HEWING CONTEMPORARY BOWLS

with

Rip & Tammi Mann

Text written with
and photography by
Douglas Congdon-Martin

Schiffer Publishing Ltd

77 Lower Valley Road, Atglen, PA 19310

M000009409

Contents

Copyright © 1995 by Rip & Tammi Mann

Library of Congress Cataloging-in-Publication Data

Mann, Rip.
    Hewing contemporary bowls with Rip & Tammi Mann / text
written with and photography by Douglas Congdon-Martin.
      p. cm. -- (A Schiffer book for woodcarvers)
    ISBN 0-88740-710-2 (softcover)
    1. Wood-carving. 2. Bowls (Tableware) I. Mann, Tammi.
II. Congdon-Martin, Douglas. III. Title. IV. Series.
TT199.7.M363   1994
736'.4--dc20   94-24311
                           CIP

All rights reserved. No part of this work may be reproduced or
used in any forms or by any means – graphic, electronic or
mechanical, including photocopying or information storage and
retrieval systems – without written permission from the copyright
holder.

Printed in China
ISBN: 0-88740-710-2

Published by Schiffer Publishing, Ltd.
77 Lower Valley Road
Atglen, PA 19310
Please write for a free catalog.
This book may be purchased from the publisher.
Please include $2.95 postage.
Try your bookstore first.

We are interested in hearing from authors
with book ideas on related subjects.

Hewing the Bowl

Bowl slabs are cut from a section of a tree approximatley 4" longer that the finished length of the bowl. The slabs are cut with the grain of the wood, *not* cross-grain.

You can see that we have removed enough sapwood, leaving a good heart-wood base.

The second cut should be parallel to the first. The thickness of the slab will determine the depth of the bowl, after the surfaces are planed smooth. Always stay 1 1/2" to 2" back from the pith.

The slab will look like this. For hewing I use green wood because it works much easier with the adze. The finishing process we use keeps the bowl from splitting or warping.

Plane both surfaces as smoothly and as parallel as possible. Once this is complete we are ready to lay out the bowl.

This is a piece of curly maple that is also spalted and wormy. It is three inches deep, and I'm going to make a twelve inch octagonal bowl out of it. You need a twelve inch square to start. Begin by scribing a line along one edge in the direction of the grain.

Draw a line across the grain.

Hold the ruler in place on that line, and, at one end, lay the square against it.

At each end of the original line, measure twelve inches to the opposite side.

Connect the marks to define the opposite side of the bowl.

The result is a twelve inch square.

Use the same method to draw the other cross grain line, measuring twelve inches from each end of the first cross grain line...

Mark the center point on each side.

and connecting the dots.

The eight sides of the octagon will have the same length. With the twelve inch square, you measure 2 1/2" out from the center marks in each direction, on the four sides of the square. If you are working with a different sized octagon you will need to experiment until you find the correct side length.

Draw a line across the corners.

At the corners you need to be aware of the direction of the grain and make your stroke with the grain.

The result. Each side of the octagon is 5 inches.

You want to come within a 1/2" of each side, but not all the way to the line.

Use the adze to knock off the corners and any excess on the other sides. In this case the slab was pretty close to size, so I didn't need to do much on the sides.

The top of the bowl roughed in.

then remove the end grain between.

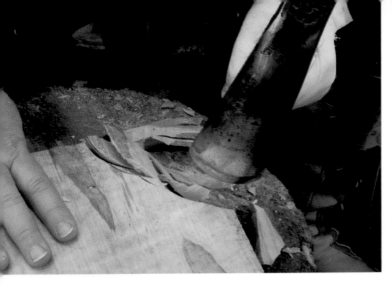

Turn the slab over and knock the corners off. When working near the edge be sure your work surface is smooth and that the edge of the bowl is in contact with it. Otherwise you will have a severe chipping problem when working along the edge of the bowl.

Repeat at the other end.

At this point, there is no measurement involved on the bottom. You want to trim enough off the corners of the bottom so that they angle out to the top. Be aware of the grain direction.

With the ends done, move to the side. With the grain running this way there is a chance you could knock the whole side off, so take small cuts, doing a little bit at a time.

Two corners done. Because end grain is so much harder to cut, I do the corners first...

On this side I have a crack, which presents a special challenge.

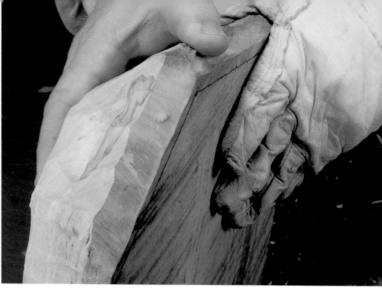

This takes you to about this position around the whole bowl. You'll notice that the top edge of the bowl is extremely thick and needs to be reduced.

To give it more strength while I'm working it I run some cyanoacrylate ester glue down the crack. This is a thin penetrating variety of super glue made particularly for wood.

Working from the bottom of the bowl, cut away another 1/2" to thin the edge.

Let the glue set-up for a few minutes, then continue your careful removal.

This should take you to about this thickness at the top edge.

When working the corner be sure to chop at an angle with the grain. Too straight and you'll chip the corner.

Progress on the bottom. Notice that I haven't come too far in yet.

Work your way around all eight surfaces.

Turn the piece over and work toward the pencil marks on the top.

This will give you a thin upper edge all around.

Go with the grain and cut right to the line.

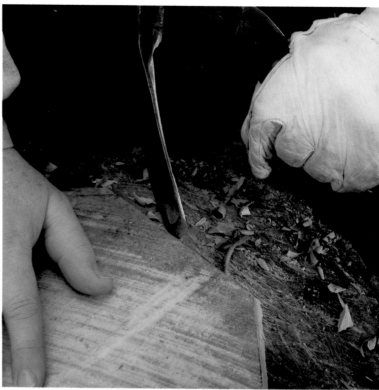

On the end grain you need to work in from both sides....

When going across the grain, a downward angled chop works better than a straight chop.

toward the middle to avoid breaking off the corner.

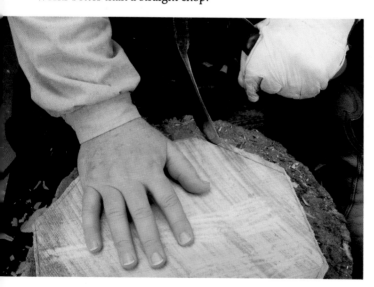

To go with the grain it is sometimes necessary to use a backhand stroke.

The top is reduced to the line.

Turn the bowl over so the top is flat against the work surface. We now need to thin the rim of the bowl again. Trim the top 1 1/2" (remember the top is against the stump now!) or so of the side plane, working toward the top edge...

so the edge is reduced to about 1/4".

All eight sides are done.

With bowl shave or a rasp make a nice, smooth edge around the top.

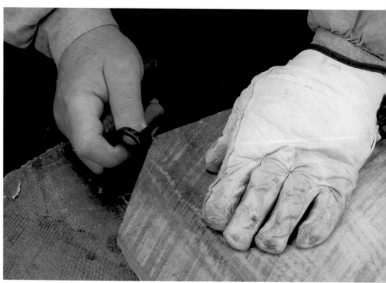

Because of the grain direction there are usually six edges of the octagon I can do with one hand and two I have to do with the other if I am to go with the grain.

We now have eight smooth edges around the top.

Turn the piece so the top is against the work surface. The bottom of the bowl is always half the diameter of the top. Since this is a twelve inch bowl, the bottom will be 6" across. To begin I lay a ruler across the bottom and butt it against a square that is flush with the top edge.

Measure in three inches and make a mark.

Move along the same edge...

Move to the next side and repeat the process...

and make another mark at three inches.

Connect the dots.

Connect the marks.

Work your way around the bottom of the bowl.

The base drawn.

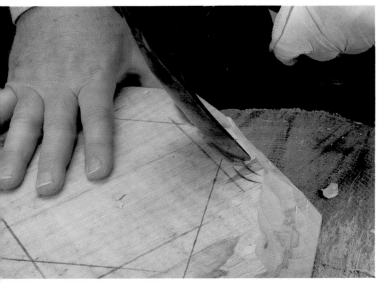

Starting a little bit back from the line, begin to reduce the side of the bowl. Remember, the sides of the octagon will not be straight.

The surfaces of the sides will have a slight curve to them. It will look roughly like this. You can see that the rim of the bow is fairly thick. It needs to be reduced to about 1/4" thickness.

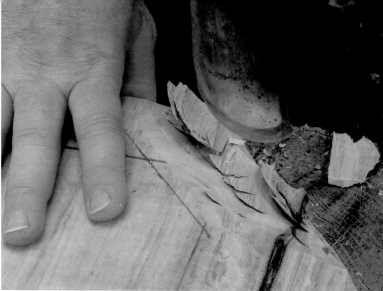

To accomplish this I am hewing only about halfway from the bottom of the side to the top. This also helps establish the curve.

Work your way around the bowl being careful when going with the grain so you don't cut off too much, and when going across the grain to cut at an angle.

The bottom roughed in.

Hew to the line, defining the bottom of the bowl. Notice the angle of the adz. Do not chop downward.

Continue all around the bottom line. Remember to chop with the grain.

The result.

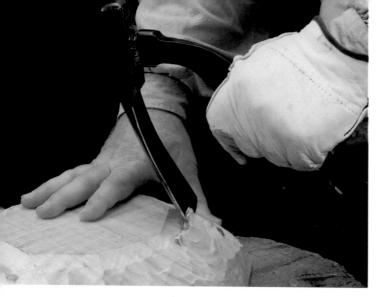

Next do a rough shaping of the sides. Start at the bottom of the bowl and, taking small bits, work toward the top (which is against the work surface).

If you review the previous photos you will see that the curve is established by the changing angle of the adze.

Work from side-to-side across a segment...

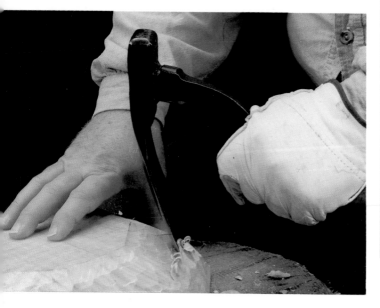

coming down about a half-inch with each row of cuts.

A side roughed in. Continue all around the bowl. Notice the thickness of the rim, roughly 1/4".

Progress.

A flexible piece of cardboard allows you to draw a guideline from the point of the bottom octagon to the point of the top rim. This will help you keep the sides even and lines straight as you do your finish hewing.

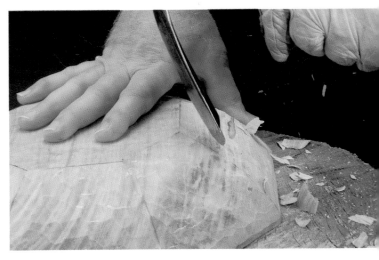

I find it is easier to start the final shaping on a side grain. Because the end grain is harder to carve you have a tendency to leave a much bigger curve. So establish the curve on the side grain and carry it around. Taking little chops, start at the bottom and work down to the top, going along the line.

Continue down to the top.

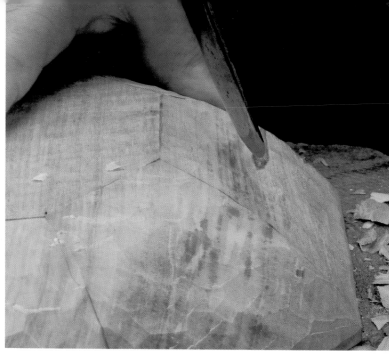

Clean out the area between the two previous cuts. Use short strokes for this final shaping.

Do the same along the other line of the segment.

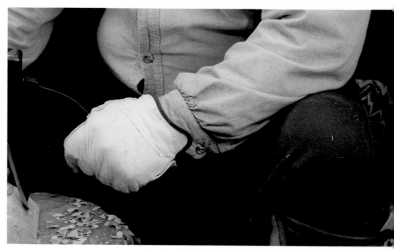

You'll find that for these short finishing strokes you'll get more control if you rest your arm on your leg.

These two cuts establish the curve of the segment. Leave about an eighth inch edge along the rim of the bowl.

By looking across the surface of the segment...

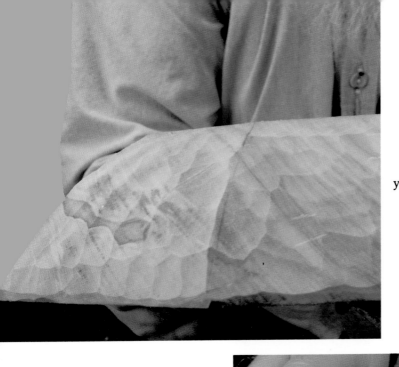

you can see the curve and spot any problems.

The edge at the top of the bowl is still intact, and is about 1/8" thick.

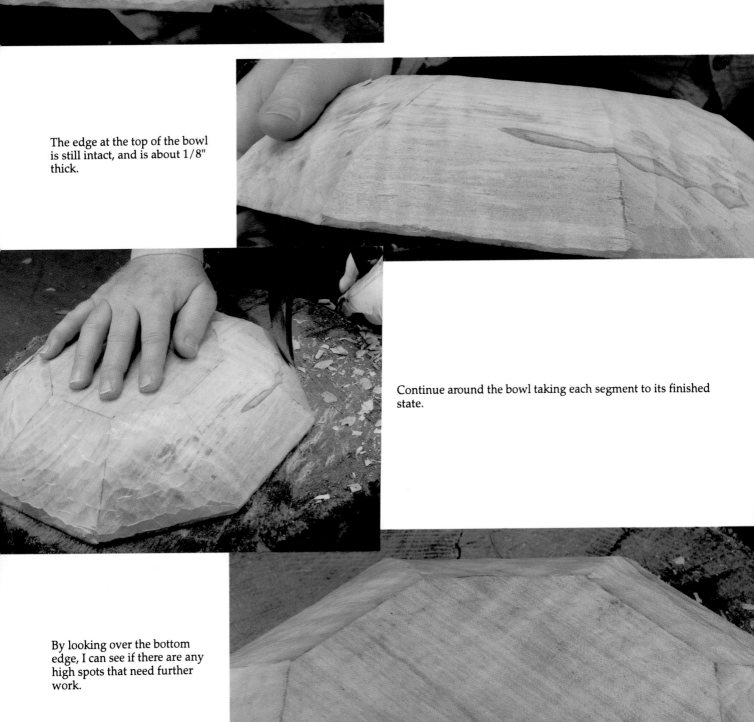

Continue around the bowl taking each segment to its finished state.

By looking over the bottom edge, I can see if there are any high spots that need further work.

The sides shaped.

Use a scorp to clean up the bottom.

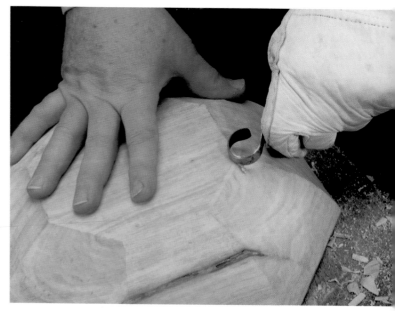

Continue with the scorp and bevel the edges around the bottom of the bowl. Remember to go with the grain.

Take off the sharp edges of the ridges between the sections.

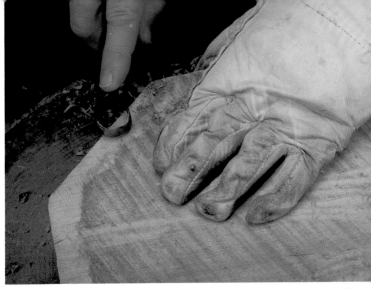

You'll need to change direction to go with the grain. Going against the grain will cause it to kick up.

This softens all the edges on the outside of the bowl.

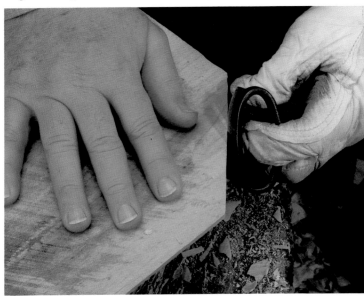

Go over the rim of the top with a bowl shave, rasp or plane.

Turn the bowl upright and clean around the edge with the scorp. You want a smooth border about 1" wide all around the top.

All the edges should now be approximately the same.

Going with the grain, round off the corners.

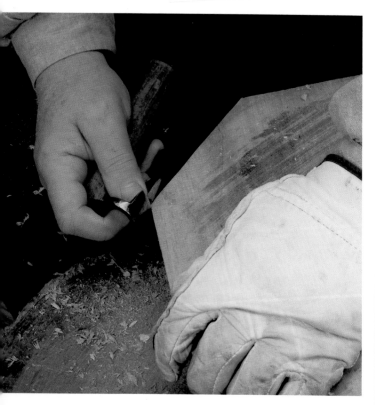

Again, going with the grain will mean changing direction for half of the corners.

This should take you to this point.

Go with the grain to bevel the top edge.

On each side, measure 5/8" in from one end...

and the other.

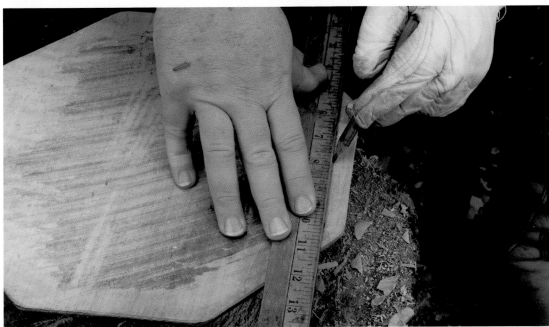

Connect
the marks.

Continue all around to define
the thickness of the lip.

Starting in the middle, cut across the grain...

at the other end of the center, again cutting across the grain.

and moving 1/2" toward the outside, cut back to it to chip out a relief line.

Between these two lines, cut with the grain to take out the waste. Cut one way...

Repeat the process...

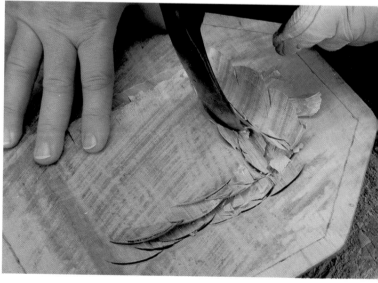

and come back to it.

Do the same thing...

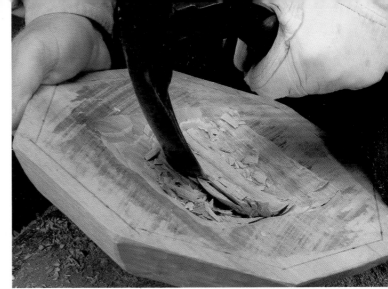

As you reach the center you can tilt the bowl up to get a better cutting angle.

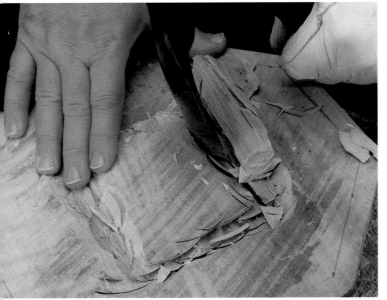

on the other side.

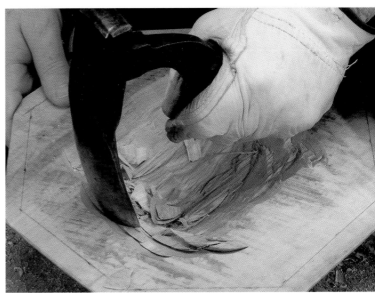

Return to cutting cross grain. Move out about 1/2" further...

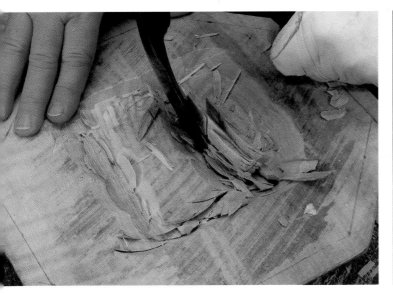

Continue the process as you work your way across the center of the bowl.

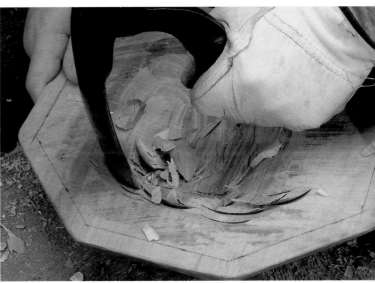

and turn the corner as your widen the cut.

Repeat at each end. Then move to cutting with the grain and clean out the center.

Tilt the bowl and clean out the bottom.

Gradually this process will bring out the eight sides of the inside of the bowl.

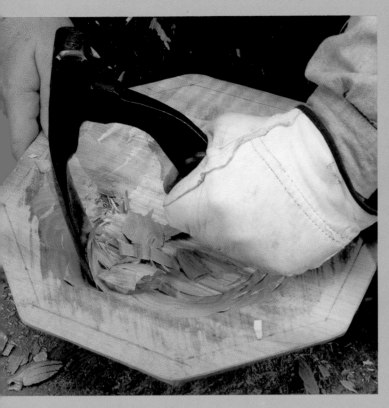

Continue to work your way out from the center. Here I've moved out another 1/2" or so.

I'm going to come across here and cut the end grain fibers.

Before cutting the side grain...

Cut the end grain to about here...

then cut the side grain.

About now is a good time to check the depth of the bowl. You want to end up with about 1/2" thickness at the bottom. To measure progress take the bowl's overall height. Here it is about 2 3/4". That means we'll need a depth of 2 1/4" on the inside to get the 1/2" thickness.

Lay a straightedge across the top of the bowl, and move the ruler to the inside of the bowl. I see that it is now 1 5/8" deep, so I have a little ways to go.

At this point I need to be a little more careful. I need to angle my cuts so they go with the grain. I need to keep aware of the depth of the bowl. And I need to remember that the outside wall, which I am trying to match, is curved.

Take smaller cuts from here on out.

Again, before cutting with the grain, cut across the grain at the corner to prevent tearing.

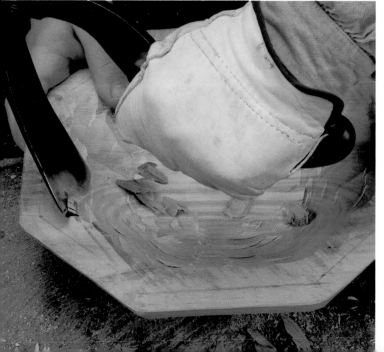

Continue shaping the sides.

Work your way all around...

Gradually move to the lines of the lip. The sides are beginning to curve, but I didn't go any deeper during the last series of cuts.

then remove the waste in the bottom.

Cut around the bottom starting with the cross grain. You want to go 1/4" to 3/8" deeper, but not to the bottom.

Thinning the sides to the proper thickness begins on one of the corner segments. This allows me to cut the fibers of grain for the long-grain side. In the first go-a-round I only go about 1" down the sides, hewing to the line.

Next I move to the end grain, taking small chops at an angle.

Do the other corner. Repeat on the other two corners and end grain before doing the sides.

The last two segments are the sides. Following this order nicely cuts the fibers at the ends of the grain.

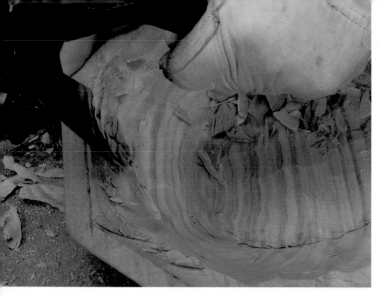

Now you can clean up the sides.

Be very careful of the end grain because it is somewhat fragile at this point in the work and can easily split.

With the first inch or so taken to size...

At this point it is a good idea to measure the bottom again.

I can go back and continue the curve of the wall into the bottom.

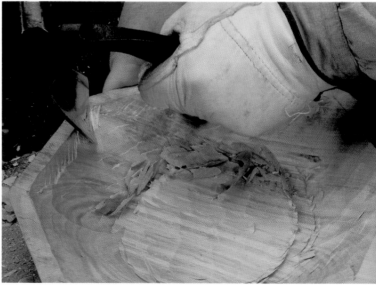

A final hewing takes away the pencil mark.

Progress.

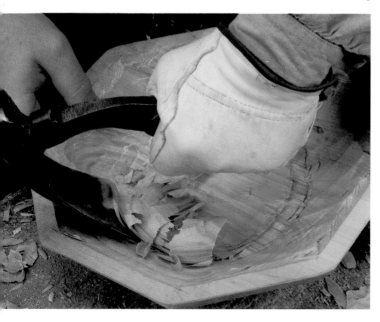

Make a final cut of the walls, carrying the curved surface to the bottom.

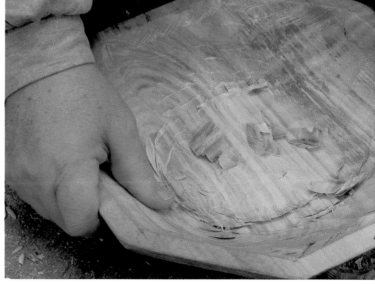

I use the fingers of my non-chopping hand to hold and to measure the thickness and uniformity of the wall as I work my way around.

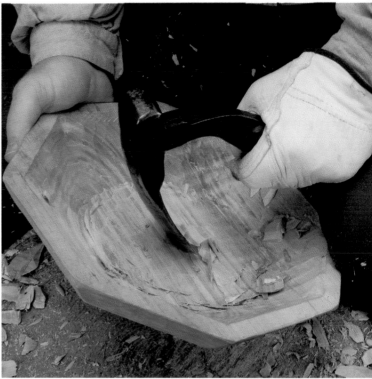

When working on the end grain, I lift up the opposite side with my leg. This changes the angle of the chop so that it creates less stress on the wood. The angle of the chop and the angle of the wood are nearly the same.

Clean up the bottom, making it more even, and around the edges where the walls and the bottom meet. Be careful not to chop into the sidewalls. There isn't enough wood there now to allow you to fix your mistake.

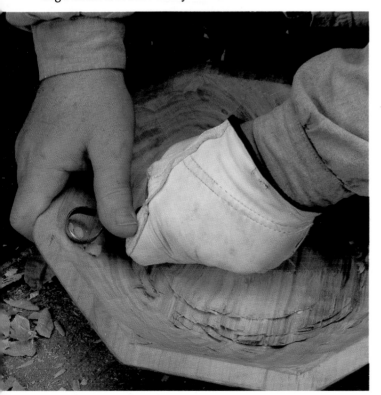

I use a scorp in the corners to clean them up and get a rounded shape that matches the outside of the bowl.

Instead, stop short of the edge and come back the other way.

Cleaning up makes it much easier to see what you have around the edges.

Thinning the sides continues. Come down one corner...

the other...

and then remove the wood in between.

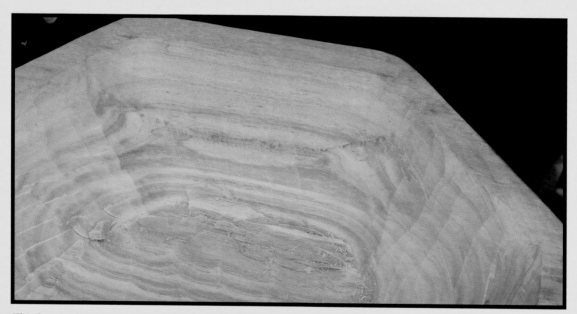

This leaves the side smoother and thinner. Remember, use shorter, finer strokes and do not go too deep into the bottom.

Looking down the edge will help you spot any problems with thicknesses in the walls.

Ready for the final hewing.

Take short controlled strokes. Remember, these strokes are easier if you support your arm on your leg.

I use the corner of the adze to pull the corner of the bowl to the bottom.

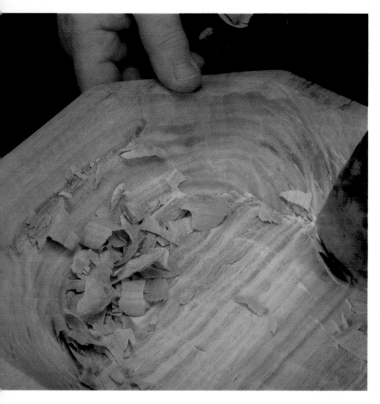

Again, on the side I've worked the ends to cut the fibers, and now am ready to take the surface down.

Use the scorp to clean up any roughness in the corners.

This side finished. Continue to work the remaining sides. Remember to try to match the inside curvature to the outside, and to align the inside and outside corners of each face.

Ready to do the bottom.

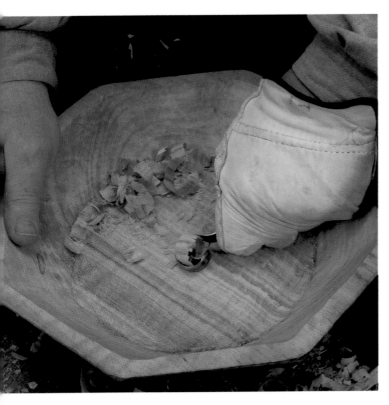

Start cleaning the bottom by going across the grain with the scorp. You want to level it and make it a little smoother.

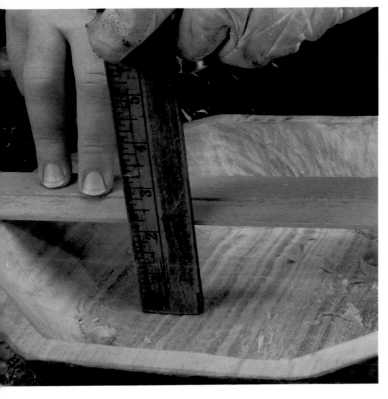

A check of the depth tells me I have just a little bit to go.

The scorp also establishes the smooth transition from side to bottom.

Continue going across the grain until you are basically finished.

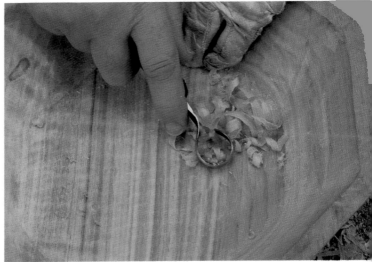

Finish by going with the grain, using the longest strokes you can.

Ready for seasoning.

Storing An Unfinished Bowl

closing the end to keep the moisture in.

Most People can't finish hewing a bowl in one day. In order to keep the bowl in good condition between your hewing sessions, wrap it in a plastic bag. Pour a small amount of water in the bottom of the bowl. This keeps it from losing moisture and the consequent cracking. You will find that most of the water is absorbed by the wood.

Store in a cool dark place until you are ready to work on it again.

Place it in a plastic bag...

Remove the bowl from the bag.

Finishing the Bowl

Preparation

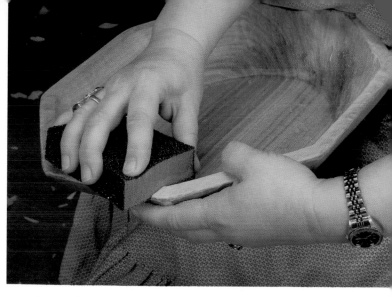

Use the flexibility of the sponge to do the surface and the inner edge of the rim at the same time. The rim is the first thing a person (customer) touches when examining a bowl, so make it feel real nice.

For closing the grain I use a medium/coarse sanding sponge. Steel wool can be used if you prefer. You do not want to remove the tool marks on this type of the bowl. They are part of its beauty and charm.

Any bowl with corners requires special attention. The grain shifts here and you need to be sure the grain is laying flat and smooth.

Start on the outside of the rim with a light sanding using the medium grit side of the sponge. With some woods, like walnut, you will need to go over it twice. If so, use the coarse grit side for the first sanding.

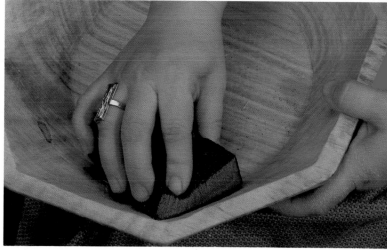

The flexibility of the sponge is helpful again when you do the inside walls.

At the transition between the wall and the bottom use the corner of the sponge.

With imperfections in the wood you also need to take extra care. Work it until it is pleasing to the touch.

The curly grain of the maple requires special care because it goes in odd directions. Check it by touch, and work it until you are satisfied.

Continue with the sides...

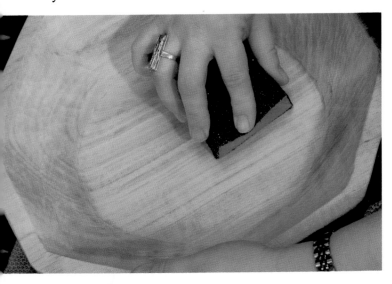

Sand the bottom of bowl.

and the bottom.

When the surfaces are complete go over each ridge.

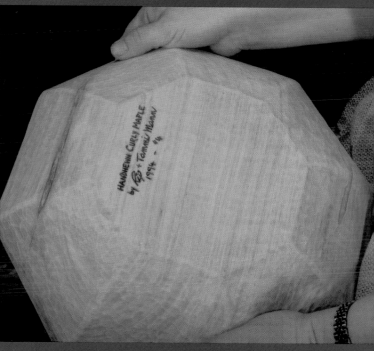

Include the wood and your signature on your work. I also include the bowl number and the year.

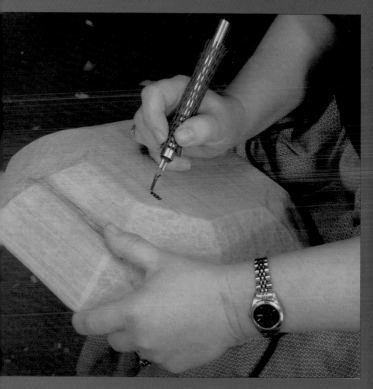

For signing the bowl with the burner I hold the bowl so that it is cross grain. The burner goes with the grain.

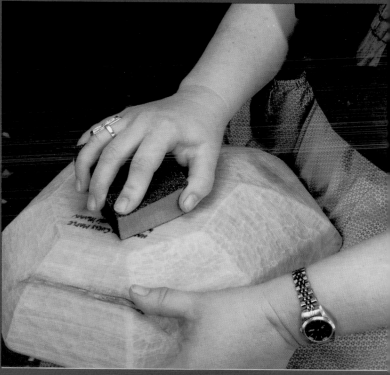

Sand over the signature, just enough to remove the rough edges.

Seasoning

1. Oil the bowl liberally, coating all surfaces completely, and paying close attention to the end grain. Put the oiled bowl into a plastic bag, closing the end tightly. The bowl sits in the bag in a cool dark space for 12 hours. Be sure it is fully supported on a flat surface.

2. Take it out of the bag, allow the water that has beaded up to evaporate (approximately 20-30 minutes). Then liberally oil the wood again. Leave it out of the bag for 12 hours, checking every hour or so to see if it needs more oil, especially the end grains. Reoil as needed during the day.

3. At the end of the twelve hours, oil liberally and place the bowl back in the bag for another twelve hours.

4. Repeat this process for the next three to five days. You will notice that the bowl requires less and less oiling during the twelve hours it is out of the bag. Denser woods will take longer than less dense woods.

5. At the end of the five days you will no longer need the bag. Leave the bowl in the same cool place and check daily to see if it needs more oiling. Some woods, like walnut, feather up with oiling. After a month or so of seasoning it is helpful to go over the bowl with a light sanding.

6. The seasoning takes approximately six weeks, during which the bowl stays in the cool dark place. Then the bowl is seasoned. It can be used for food use and put in the house. I recommend reoiling every six months, on Father's Day and Christmas. After use you may wipe out the bowl with a hot sudsy cloth, rinsing and drying immediately. If especially messy, you can clean the bowl in the sink, but don't let it soak in the water. Rinse and dry immediately.

7. Don't leave the bowl on top of the refrigerator or in direct sunlight, or other places where heat or light may damage it.

Pour 3-4 tablespoons of peanut oil in the bottom of the bowl.

Work a liberal coating of the oil over all the surfaces.

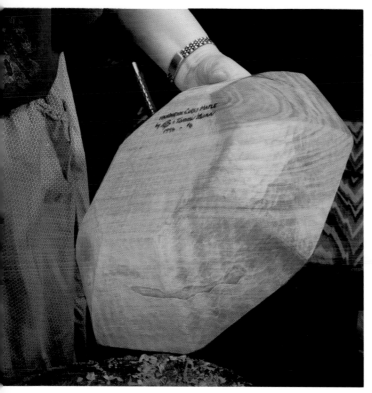

The oil brings the grain alive.

Place the bowl in a plastic bag to season it.

Twist the opening of the bag to keep the air in.

Cover the outside of the bowl.

Fold the end under the bowl and set the bowl aside to let the oil work in.

The Gallery of
Hewn Bowls

Curly Maple Octagon. *From the collection of Mr. & Mrs. Jim Good.*

Black Walnut Octagon. *From the collection of Karin Schmidt.*

Wormy Maple Modern
Applachian Rectangle
*From the collection of
Deb & Jim Roberson.*

Spalted Beech
Fluted Bowl.
*From the artist's
personal collection.*

Sassafras Heart. *From the collection of* Diane Corn.

Black Walnut Double Heart

Curly Maple Double Heart. *From the collection of Bill & Judy Chandler.*

Wormy Maple "Texas". *From the artist's personal collection.*

Wild Cherry "Virginia". *From the artist's personal collection.*

Figured Cherry Crotch Freeform. *From the collection of Angela Mann.*

Burled Chinese Elm. *From the collection of Donn & Bunny Railey.*

Wild Cherry Sandwich Plates and Salad Bowl Sets.
From the collection of Tram & Melba Lance.